Battling
for the
Light
Overcomer's Series

M. J. Welcome

Other Books by M. J. Welcome:

Overcome Secret Sins in 15 Days

Smart Publishing House
Division of MDW Consulting Group
Far Rockaway, NY 11691
www.smartpublishinghouse.com

© 2015 Michelle J. Dyett-Welcome. All rights reserved.

No Part of this book may be reproduced, stored in retrieval system, or transmitted by any means without the written permission of the author.

First Published by Smart House Publishing 12/11/15

ISBN-13: 978-0692599723
ISBN-10: 069259972X

Printed in the United States of America
Far Rockaway, New York

This book is printed on acid-free paper

Table of Contents

APPRECIATION v

INTRODUCTION vii

WARRIOR OF LIGHT xiii

DAY 1 WE WRESTLE AGAINST 1

DAY 2 FROM HENCEFORTH BRETHEREN 9

DAY 3 TIME TO GET DRESSED 15

DAY 4 TAKE UNTO YOU 21

DAY 5 YOUR LOINS GIRT ABOUT WITH TRUTH 27

DAY 6 PREPARATION OF THE GOSPEL OF PEACE 31

DAY 7 TAKE UP THE SHIELD OF FAITH 37

DAY 8 IT'S TIME TO TAKE 44

DAY 9 PRAYING ALWAYS 50

DAY 10 CHILDREN OF LIGHT 61

DAY 11 LET YOUR LIGHT SO SHINE 70

DAY 12 CANDLES HIDE NOT 77

DAY 13 WHILE YE HAVE LIGHT 84

DAY 14 YE ARE ALL CHILDREN OF LIGHT 90

DAY 15 LIGHT SHINETH IN DARKNESS 95

CONCLUSION 102

APPRECIATION

Greetings in the name of our Lord and Savior Jesus Christ! God is a good and faithful God. His love is astounding and His patience toward the children of men is unfathomable. To Him be all glory, honor and praise now and forever. Amen.

I am grateful to God for His many blessings in my life, my family, my health, and for a making a way for me to have a sound mind through Christ Jesus.

Special thanks goes to my critique buddies who tirelessly helped me to polish this devotional, may the Lord continue to bless you according to his riches in glory through Christ Jesus.

I'm also thankful for you. It is my earnest prayer that God will magnify Himself in your life and that you will declare that He has done something new in you as you battle for the **LIGHT**!

INTRODUCTION

This book is not a comprehensive work, nor is it the final word on biblical understanding. By the grace of Jesus as administered by the power of Holy Spirit, we will take a closer look at the deeper meaning of certain scriptures. God challenges us to search and study his word.

> *"Study to shew thyself approved unto God, a workman that needeth not to be ashamed, rightly dividing the word of truth."*
>
> *2 Timothy 2:15*

Revelation, understanding and increased spiritual knowledge is the food of those who are willing to inquire of the Lord. It is for those who make it their quest in life to get to know their God. God has chosen to hide things. This act of God weeds out the lazy, the disinterested, the rebellious and the wicked.

> *"It is the glory of God to conceal a thing: but the honour of kings is to search out a matter."*
>
> *Proverbs 25:2*

Once we have understanding, revelation, and wisdom we are expected to exercise our senses to discern good and evil and constantly choose the good.

> *"But strong meat belongeth to them that are of full age, even those who by reason of use have their senses exercised to discern both good and evil."*
>
> *Hebrews 5:14*

Therefore, as you read, choose the good. Anything that does not resonate with you ask Holy Spirit to be the revealer of truth. Let God be the final authority.

"Prove all things; hold fast that which is good."

1 Thessalonians 5:21

"Howbeit when he, the Spirit of truth, is come, he will guide you into all truth: for he shall not speak of himself; but whatsoever he shall hear, that shall he speak: and he will shew you things to come."

John 16:13

The Apostle Paul tells us in Ephesians 6:12 that we wrestle with principalities, powers, rulers of darkness, and spiritual wickedness in high places. Their objective is to blanket the earth with darkness as they eliminate every source of light. They want to return the world to its pre-creation state, when the world was void and without form.

> *"And the earth was without form, and void; and darkness was upon the face of the deep. And the Spirit of God moved upon the face of the waters."*
>
> Genesis 1:2
>
> *"I beheld the earth, and, lo, it was without form, and void; and the heavens, and they had no light."*
>
> Jeremiah 4:23

When we examine the Hebrew meaning of Genesis 1:2, we learn that the world was full of confusion, emptiness, obscurity, and darkness, which concealed light. The earth was a literal wasteland. By filling the earth with darkness Satan and his followers hoped to diminish or conceal light in order to remove the pollute God's creation.

Today their desire is to cause many to fall short of the glory of God for they know the Great and terrible day of the Lord is soon at hand.

> *"Behold, he cometh with clouds; and every eye shall see him, and they also which pierced him: and all kindreds of the earth shall wail because of him. Even so, Amen."*

Revelation 1:7

> *"Therefore rejoice, ye heavens, and ye that dwell in them. Woe to the inhabiters of the earth and of the sea! for the devil is come down unto you, having great wrath, because he knoweth that he hath but a short time."*

Revelation 12:12

If Satan can corrupt believers causing our lights to become dim or if he turns God's children into children of darkness then he would have succeed in disqualifying us as children of light. Thus reducing the amount of light, which radiates in the earth while increasing the level of darkness.

The light of Christ Jesus is vital for it *transforms* us individually, but it also exposes and convicts the world of sin.

It is our duty as believers to battle for the light, to radiate from within the splendor and brilliance of Christ, and to emanate light throughout the earth by the things we do, speak, plan, implement, desire, crave, and hope for.

Here's to *your* **VICTORY** as you battle for the LIGHT!

M.J. Welcome

WARRIOR OF LIGHT

As believers we're called to be warriors of light. It's our responsibility to shed light wherever we go and to displace *all* darkness. We are to be active and ever advancing the banner of Jesus Christ.

But do we truly understand the call that has been placed on us? Do we properly discern the awesome responsibility entrusted to us?

The Hebrew word for **warrior** is *can'an,* which means to tread or to trample. It also means a shoe that protects our feet from clay and mud. Therefore, a warrior is one who treads or tramples in clayey or miry ground with protected feet.

Furthermore, as warriors we are commissioned to be lights in dark places (Matthew 5:14, John 12:46, John 1:5, and Isaiah 42:16), and to live as children of light (1 Thessalonians 5:5, Ephesians 5:8, and Ephesians 4:17-32).

But what does it mean to be light, to emit light, or to advance light? Or to be a warrior of light?

The Hebrew word for **light** is **'owr** which means light, light of day, or light of heavenly luminaries. It also includes lightning (Luke 10:18), lamp (Luke 11:33), to kindle (in the negative sense as in Isaiah 50:11), to lighten (the eyes as in 2 Kings 6:17, or in the sense of God's law as in Nehemiah 8:8). It means to shine, with pleasantness or cheerfulness of countenance (Act 6:15).

As we examine the word **'owr** further we discover that it also means Jehovah as Israel's light (likewise God's anointed King David 2 Samuel 21:17), the light of life, instruction, the face (Exodus 34:35), prosperity, doctrine, teaching, and the light of life (Jesus).

"Then spoke Jesus again unto them, saying, I am the light of the world: he that follows me shall not walk in darkness, but shall have the light of life."

John 8:12

"In him was life; and the life was the light of men."

John 1:4

"Jesus saith unto him, I am the way, the truth, and the life: no man cometh unto the Father, but by me."

John 14:6

When we put the words together, we notice that ***a warrior of light*** is one who establishes light in every corner of life by trampling or treading on darkness. He is radiant, pleasant, and cheerful. He instructs, and shares the doctrines of God. He is vested in the prosperity of others, not only on an earthly, monetary, or material level but on a spiritual level, which manifests itself in the natural as it fulfills an eternal and heavenly objective.

A warrior of light is committed to advancing the kingdom of God. He seeks after it first (Matthew 6:33). He desires to teach and convert transgressors.

> "Then will I teach transgressors thy ways; and sinners shall be converted unto thee."
>
> Psalms 51:13

A warrior confronts darkness with courage, faith, and determination clothed in the armor of light.

The armor of God ensures that the warrior will not be soiled, ensnared, or lose his footing as he wages war against the foe(s) of God (Psalms 18:46-48).

Our objective is to subdue all rebels under the feet of God (Luke 20:42-43), reclaim the territory which was carried off into captivity by the enemy, spread out and claim new territory for our God, and to establish light where ever we go.

Our duty is to exercise the authority of Christ on the earth (Matthew 28:18, Luke 10:19, Matthew 18:18, and Matthew 16:19) and help usher in the sovereign rule of the King of Kings (Revelation 21:2)!

Are you ready for WAR?

DAY 1

WE WRESTLE AGAINST

> *"For we wrestle not against flesh and blood, but against principalities, against powers, against the rulers of the darkness of this world, against spiritual wickedness in high places."*
>
> Ephesians 6:12

In Ephesians 6:12, Paul clearly distinguishes the parties at war. On one side, there is man (believers) and on the other are principalities, powers, rulers, and spiritual wickedness. But what is the distinguishing mark between the sides?

Man, is distinguished by the soft substance of skin, that covers the bones and is permeated with blood. He

Battling for the Light

is the being that was the original property of God and was carried off into captivity, sin, and death as the spoils of another.

Furthermore, he was separated from the place of spiritual life or total existence in God because of sin.

Principalities, the first enemy mentioned by Paul is a rebel state or place under the rulership of a fallen spiritual prince (without flesh, bones, or blood). It was and is the first of its kind (chief entity) in a series of states. It was the first to commence a thing according to the Greek meaning of ***principalities***.

In essence, it's a government set up by spiritual criminals to rule over an area. Their primary objective was and is to lead, rule, originate new beginnings, and to exercise dominion over the inhabitants under the rule of the state.

The next group is ***powers***, the Greek meaning of powers reveals to us how they accomplish their objectives. They do as they please, by exercising physical and mental power, demonstrating ability, strength, and authority over those who are under their state or governmental rule. Those over whom they rule must obey their commands for they have a legal right or jurisdiction over them, which originates from the principality or chief state.

In essence they force their will upon the inhabitants of their state (2 Timothy 2:26).

Next, Paul reveals whom these beings are that exercise dominion and set up spiritual states. They are the ***rulers of darkness of this world***, which are comprised of the prince of this age (also known as the lord of this world, or the devil) and his coconspirators. He and his band of thieves carry men (the original possessions of God) way into captivity at his will (2 Timothy 2:26).

The rulers are hostile to the cause of Christ and they diligently work against the purposes of God by aggravating things in the earth realm. They interfere with world affairs and earthy goods. They stir up desires and fleeting pleasures in an attempt to seduce men from God or to keep them in bondage. In so doing, they are able to secure their rulership over the minds and lives of men, thus becoming their master (Romans 6:16).

But how are the *rulers* able to execute such a successful coup which spans centuries?

They implore the use of darkness. They blind people to truth. They clothe the captives in ignorance to divine things and sweeten it with ungodliness and immorality. At first, they block or intercept the light of truth, snatching it away from man (Matthew 13:19).

Then they methodically and diabolically woo man down a path of unrighteousness until he is held in check by his own ignorance, foolish thoughts, perverted desires, lusts, or depravities thus ensuring he will be together with them (the rulers) in the misery of hell.

Paul puts to bed any notion that the rulers could be alien invaders or galactic travelers. They are *of this world*. They are bound in a real and tangible sense to this planet and are not free to surf the galaxies in order to invade or contaminate other atmospheric regions. So for an unbroken age, a perpetuity of time they have been allowed to rule on earth, over the inhabitants of the earth, and over worldly affairs, that was, until Christ came to reestablish divine order (1 John 3:8 and Colossians 2:15).

The final group are *spiritual wickedness in high places*. This group pertains to human entities, the human spirit or rational soul. These are the men that were born to the daughters of men that are part human and part spiritual beings (Genesis 6:1-4). These beings are higher than man is but lower than God, they are demons, familiar, or evil spirits.

Battling for the Light

They are full of depravity, malice, and evil purposes. Their assignment is to stir up annoyances, perils, pain, trouble, and hard labor for man. They cause physical manifestations of disease, blindness, deafness, and deformities. There is no good in them! They exist for one purpose to destroy everything that God desires to exist. They want to make men poor in mind, body, and soul causing them to be spiritually bankrupt transforming them into the "living dead."

Paul doesn't leave us guessing as to where these entities exist. Some reside in the vaulted expanse of the sky where all things are visible to them (fallen angels). And others (the demons) reside in mountains or elevated areas.

Our fight is against eternal spiritual governments, that were set up from when Satan was flung out of heaven. We fight against their authority in order to establish Christ's dominion over the earth and give the residents therein an opportunity to choose *life*.

> *"The thief cometh not, but for to steal, and to kill, and to destroy: I am come that they might have life, and that they might have it more abundantly."*
>
> John 10:10

We battle against the devil, his cohorts, and the evil spirits breed from the unholy union of rebellious angels and the daughters of fallen men in order to usher in the kingdom of God on the earth.

> *"Thy kingdom come. Thy will be done in earth, as it is in heaven."*
>
> Matthew 6:10

These are the things we are called to battle against. Are you ready to wage war for the kingdom of God?

Battling for the Light

Time to Examine Thyself

Are there areas in your life which the devil still uses to pull you into captivity at his will? Are you fully aligned with the kingdom of light in all areas of your life? Are you ready to exercise authority over these areas or entities by the power of God?

Pray

Lord give me the grace to break every stronghold of the enemy in my life. Increase my faith, give me strength, and make me steadfast and immovable so that I can wage war against the kingdom of Satan to the glory of God.

Let me not be covered in shame. Let me not operate in treason. Robe me in the righteousness of Jesus Christ and may every battle be declared a victory, every skirmish a triumph, and every opposing force defeated and removed from my life in Jesus name, amen!

Overcomer's Series

DAY 2

FROM HENCEFORTH BRETHEREN

> *Finally, my brethren, be strong in the Lord, and in the power of his might.*
>
> Ephesians 6:10

Brethren, from henceforth forsake the inferior life, the one full of lack, wanting, and failure, leave it behind. Choose rather to receive strength from the Spirit of God through Christ Jesus!

In Ephesians 6:10, Paul gives sound instruction on how to change our lives forever. As his brethren we are united by a bond of affection in Christ. We are employed by the same Master in order to carry out God's divine will in our lives and on the earth.

Battling for the Light

In order to accomplish the work set before us, our past ways have to be abandoned. It was and is inferior to the task ahead of us. In order to accomplish God's spiritual work we have to forsake natural means, measures, and tools through the grace of Jesus.

Furthermore, we need to consent and agree to God's complete process by submitting our will to Him through Christ Jesus. Jesus is to be Lord over us.

According to the Greek meaning of the word **Lord**, it is one who has power of deciding, one to whom a person, or thing belongs. Therefore, as believers we are the property of Jesus, he has the power of decision over our lives. He gets to decide if we live or die.

Yet Jesus is not a dictator, his Lordship over our lives and circumstances is contingent on our continued consent and agreement. His lordship requires us to submit to him as he submitted to the will of God the Father (Matthew 12:50, John 6:38, and Matthew 7:21).

Overcomer's Series

At any time we don't agree or consent we have removed ourselves from the vine and are on our own. In order to bear spiritual fruit we are to remain connected to Christ (John 15:4). If we desire to be victorious, we must remain attached to the one who possesses the power of God.

Power resides in Jesus by virtue of his nature. When we abide in him, we are endued with spiritual strength, we are caused to become strong and powerful in him so that we can take dominion over the works, plans, devise, schemes, and plots of the enemy.

In the beginning, the world was full of darkness and chaos (Genesis 1:1-2). The Word of God released power and took dominion over the earth manifesting creation (Genesis 1). He released divine order. This same process which is available to us if we remain connected to Jesus. God's divine order will be manifested in our lives.

Battling for the Light

No longer will failure or inferiority be our portion. We will not exist by the lower denser air but by the higher air of the Spirit. We will breathe in the breath of God and live in a higher atmospheric region (Ephesians 2:6) as citizens of the kingdom of God (Ephesians 2:19).

In order to fulfill the work assigned to us we need Jesus. Without him we will experience continual disappointment and failure (Matthew 17:19-20).

But with him . . .

> *"I can do all things through Christ which strengtheneth me."*
>
> Philippians 4:13

Overcomer's Series

Hereafter, let us choose to remain, rest, and abide in Jesus, the possessor of divine power, spiritual might, the exposer and disposer of every evil work of the enemy, amen.

Are you ready for war?

Battling for the Light

Time to Examine Thyself

Are you truly the property of Christ? Does he have sovereign power over your life?

Do you trust him with your life? Are you willing to die if he deems it good for his eternal purposes? Are you fully living the superior life God purposed for you?

Pray

Lord I desire to live the superior life in you. I want to live the total will of God for my life.

My life is not my own it was purchased with a price (1 Corinthians 6:20 and 1 Corinthians 7:23) for it is not I that lives but you who lives in me (Galatians 2:19-20).

Lord give me the grace to order my life as you desire, amen.

Overcomer's Series

DAY 3

TIME TO GET DRESSED

> *"Put on the whole armour of God, that ye may be able to stand against the wiles of the devil."*
>
> Ephesians 6:11

The phrase **put on** in Ephesians 6:11, conveys more than one might think. Paul's use of these words is deliberate. He wanted to inform believers that they are to sink into the armor of God as if sinking into garments.

The Greek meaning of **put on** also means to go towards, come out from, or move away from, enter into or be plunge into something. If we apply the fullness of the phrase to Ephesians 6:11, we understand that Paul was indicating that when we **put on** the armor of God we are entering into something different from what was before. We are moving in toward a

Battling for the Light

new place of being or existing. We are leaving something behind and plunging into a new existence.

The armor of God is unlike earthly or natural garments they can't be torn, worn out, faded, or damaged by careless use, mismanagement, or attacks from the enemy but they can diminish in glory and they can be soiled or tarnished by inappropriate use.

Manmade garments degrade over time but the garments of God are eternal and endued with supernatural ability to weather storms and to prevail in every circumstance provided the wearer lives a life of subjection to the ways and counsel of God in the righteousness of Jesus.

When we use the armor of God by faith, the enemy's fiery darts are quenched. Satan is unable to gain victory over us . . . if we are properly armed with the garments of God.

Overcomer's Series

"Above all, taking the shield of faith, wherewith ye shall be able to quench all the fiery darts of the wicked."

Ephesians 6:16

Paul gives us a stern admonishment. We are to put on the whole armor of God. It's foolish to think that we can go into battle half-dressed or equipped and believe we will come out unharmed or undefeated!

Victory is ours if we are properly adorned with the full, and complete armor of God.

We are to wear the entire collection of gear, which includes the shield, sword, helmet, breastplate, belt (girdle), (greaves), shoes, and prayer and supplication. These are the tools that God has provided for us to use as the weapons of warfare, so we may stand strong in the Lord. If we choose not to use them, we have chosen weakness and ultimately defeat.

Battling for the Light

"Finally, my brethren, be strong in the Lord, and in the power of his might."

Ephesians 6:10

Are you ready to get dressed?

Overcomer's Series

Time to Examine Thyself

How are you currently dressed? Are you wearing the full armor of God? Are you half dressed? Naked? Robed in garments of shame?

Are you ready to put on the full armor of God today?

Pray

Lord forgive me for treating your garments as common things, for believing the lies of the devil that I can wear my filthy rags and still be accepted by you.

Father, change my garments, cover me in a robe of righteousness, hide me behind the blood of Jesus, and give me the grace to know you more.

Help me to understand the wonderful gift you have given me through salvation.

Battling for the Light

And open my eyes, help me to guard against being robbed by the enemy.

Restore to me what I have squandered, replenish all that is depleted, and strengthen what is left.

Thank you for hearing and answering my request, amen (Ephesians 6:19 and Philippians 4:6).

Overcomer's Series

DAY 4

TAKE UNTO YOU

> *"Wherefore take unto you the whole armour of God, that ye may be able to withstand in the evil day, and having done all, to stand."*

Ephesians 6:13

Now that you understand the situation brethren, regarding whom we fight against (principalities, powers, rulers of darkness, and spiritual wickedness) this is the action and the grounds (channel or reasons) by which your actions should proceed.

Paul laid out an airtight case for the brethren. He had no doubt that his words would be understood.

Paul heralded an alarm, **people there's a war waging,** unlike any that you have seen, experienced, or heard of before. It's one that is fought in spiritual

Battling for the Light

realms. One in which we battle a formidable foe. There is only one way to stand against him and his government (kingdom), and only course you can reasonably take. There are no other options. It's impossible to do it on your own, with earthly weapons, or by natural tactics.

If you want to survive, remain free, and be an overcomer then follow this channel of action. ***Take unto you . . . .***

In order to follow Paul's instruction we must make a decision (a judgment) about what Paul has shared. We must determine for ourselves if his words are true, accurate, reasonable, believable, and sound. We must decide if we are willing to investigate or examine it closer by testing it out for ourselves.

The phrase ***take unto you*** means to raise something in order to carry it or use it. There is no notion of violence in the action of taking up the item but rather to claim or procure the item for one's self. It is to seize or apprehend something with the intent of not letting it go. It is laying hold of an item without the notion of rejecting or refusing it.

The root meaning of the phrase exposes the fact that a choice or selection has been made in order to prove a thing, to make a trial of the thing, or to experience a thing.

It means to receive a person and give him access to one's self. In this case, it is receiving the equipping of God that comes through the Lord Jesus and Holy Spirit and to be arrayed in the full armor of God.

> *"Behold, I stand at the door, and knock: if any man hears my voice, and opens the door, I will come in to him, and will eat with him, and he with me."*
>
> Revelation 3:20

Battling for the Light

"Jesus answered and said unto him, If a man love me, he will keep my words: and my Father will love him, and we will come unto him, and make our abode with him."

John 14:23

"But ye shall receive power, after that the Holy Ghost is come upon you: and ye shall be witnesses unto me both in Jerusalem, and in all Judaea, and in Samaria, and unto the uttermost part of the earth."

Acts 1:8

Some men are skeptics they believe only what they see, test or prove for themselves. God understands this. That is why He invites us to try it out. God is confident that His armor will do as it was created to do, to keep us standing in the midst of battle.

Overcomer's Series

Are you willing to do as Paul advises, and **take unto you** *the whole armor of God*?

If so God will prove that His armor is more than sufficient to keep you standing against the wiles of the devil. Christ himself has proved it. It will not fail. All who use it wholly and completely in faith are assured victory.

Battling for the Light

Time to Examine Thyself

What do you believe about the armor of God? Are you willing to test (prove) God? Are you willing to risk being an overcomer?

Pray

From the beginning, you intended for me to be an overcomer. You have given me all that I need to win every battle through Jesus Christ.

Father, forgive me wherein I have sinned by relying on my own wits, skills, plans, schemes, and devices. It's my desire to triumph over the enemy to the glory of God.

I want to be a light bearer in the earth. I want to lift you up so you may draw men unto yourself. I take unto myself the full armor of God; give me the grace to robe myself continually in your garments to the glory of your name and to the destruction of all opposing forces, amen.

Overcomer's Series

DAY 5

YOUR LOINS GIRT ABOUT WITH TRUTH

"Stand therefore, having your loins girt about with truth, and having on the breastplate of righteousness"

Ephesians 6:14

In Ephesians 6:14, Paul counsels us to girt our loins with truth. Why our loins? Why with truth? The loin is the area of procreative power; it is the part of the body responsible for production or reproduction in terms of offspring. By Paul's use of this word, it is evident that we are to produce or reproduce in truth.

We are admonished to fasten truth to ourselves as in a yoke on a cattle's neck. Truth is to be our foundation; it will lead, keep, and sustain us against the assaults of the enemy. The knowledge of truth will enable us to

Battling for the Light

avoid troublesome laws others try to impose on us (Galatians 5:1). Truth will keep our way lit as we live in a world of darkness (Psalms 119:105).

Truth equips us to find what is true in any matter under consideration. And it is truth that will cause us to be opposers of falsehood and deceit. It will rally us to speak out against half-truths, white lies, or shades of gray. Truth will stir us to open our mouths for what is right in God's sight.

As believers, we are to align ourselves with the origin of truth. We are to attach ourselves to Christ and no other (John 14:6 and John 15:4-5). Why?

Christ is the truth of God, he is the Word of God, and he is the light of God.

> *"Jesus saith unto him, I am the way, the truth, and the life: no man cometh unto the Father, but by me."*
>
> John 14:6

Overcomer's Series

"Then spake Jesus again unto them, saying, I am the light of the world: he that followeth me shall not walk in darkness, but shall have the light of life."

John 8:12

Therefore, as we girt ourselves in truth we fasten ourselves to life, the Word of God, to light, and his undeniable truth.

Battling for the Light

Time to Examine Thyself

What girts your loins? Are you silent in the midst of lies?

Are you secretly sympathetic when someone tells a "white lie"? Do you indulge in telling lies for a good reason or cause? Will God accept your rational for creating or tolerating lies?

> "For without are dogs, and sorcerers, and whoremongers, and murderers, and idolaters, and whosoever loveth and maketh a lie."
>
> Revelation 22:15

Pray

Father forgive me for speaking lies, condoning lies, sympathizing with liars, and making a lie. Wash me and clean me.

Lord, it is my desire that truth will be my foundation. That I will love truth above all. Girt my loins with your truth, I pray in Jesus name, amen.

Overcomer's Series

DAY 6

PREPARATION OF THE GOSPEL OF PEACE

And your feet shod with the preparation of the gospel of peace;

Ephesians 6:15

Brethren, before you go about, move your feet, walk along, or try to teach others how to walk in the ways of God shod your feet with the preparation of the gospel of peace!

Shod, what does it mean? **Preparation of the gospel of peace . . .** what was Paul instructing the brethren to do?

Battling for the Light

According to the Greek meaning of the word **shod** we are instructed to bind or tie our feet with the preparation of the gospel of peace.

Paul's words convey the importance of putting our journey under the obligation or duty of the law of grace (Romans 6:14) which is the good news of the gospel.

God has opened a door, made a way for fallen man to be reconciled with Him through grace. Grace, which is God's unmerited favor, is the prerequisite to the gospel of peace, for without it we are declared enemies of God.

> *"For if, when we were enemies, we were reconciled to God by the death of his Son, much more, being reconciled, we shall be saved by his life."*
>
> Romans 5:10

Overcomer's Series

"And you, that were sometime alienated and enemies in your mind by wicked works, yet now hath he reconciled In the body of his flesh through death, to present you holy and unblameable and unreproveable in his sight:"

Colossians 1:21-22

In Ephesians 6:15, Paul informs us that as believers we are duty bound to bind this truth to our activities. We are to be compelled by this conviction to keep it tied to our person. This truth is to under-bind us.

The law of grace is the governing factor when sharing of the gospel. It opens the way of peace with the owner of peace himself, God the Father.

If God hadn't blessed man with His grace there would be no hope for anyone to be reconciled to him inevitably there would be no hope of peace. Man would have been doomed to the same fate as Satan and his band of criminals!

Battling for the Light

In order to avoid being placed back in the yoke of bondage by the enemy, by ourselves or from others, we need to be ready, prepared, and fit for the work of the kingdom. The only way to be ready is to understand and know that peace with God comes through the gospel of Christ, which is given because God chose to give it to us. We can't earn it, can't buy it, can't bargain for it, but we can choose to receive it.

If we fail to follow the counsel of Paul, the enemy will put us back under the law which opens the way for sin to ensnare, entrap, and rule over us by stirring up desires in our mortal body (Romans 6:12-17) opening the way for every form of evil to take root and eventually manifest in our lives.

> "But those things which proceed out of the mouth come forth from the heart; and they defile the man. For out of the heart proceed evil thoughts, murders, adulteries, fornications, thefts, false witness, blasphemies: These are the things which defile a man: but to eat with unwashed hands defiles not a man."
>
> Matthew 15:18-20

Why should we be bound under the law when the gospel of Christ, the good news of God's grace, has delivered us and declared us free from sin? (Romans 6:17-18)

> "Stand fast therefore in the liberty wherewith Christ hath made us free, and be not entangled again with the yoke of bondage."
>
> Galatians 5:1

Battling for the Light

Time to Examine Thyself

Are you an ambassador of grace? Do you sow peace or strife and contention?

Are you happy when all is going well or do you come alive and energized in conflict? Are you an agent of reconciliation?

Pray

Father, fill me with love for all men so I can disperse your love in the earth. Shod my feet with peace so I can live in peace with all men (Romans 12:18 and Hebrews 12:14) to the glory of God.

Help me to be an ambassador of your grace and an agent of reconciliation. Let the light of Jesus emanate through me so that many may be drawn out of darkness and come into the light, I pray, amen.

Overcomer's Series

DAY 7

TAKE UP THE SHIELD OF FAITH

> *"Above all, taking the shield of faith, wherewith ye shall be able to quench all the fiery darts of the wicked."*

Ephesians 6:16

Paul advises believers in Ephesians 6:16, to take up the shield of faith, to carry it with them in order to use it among and in the midst of battle. Faith is the key component in our arsenal through Jesus Christ. This is emphasized by the phrase ***above all***.

Battling for the Light

The phrase **above all** notifies us that the shield of faith is before, has a higher position, and is of greater importance than the other protective gear referenced in Ephesians 6. Why? Because without it we can't please God nor will we receive anything from God (Hebrews 11:6 and James 1:7-8).

By faith in Christ Jesus we are able to stand against the enemy with confidence, we can uphold the truth of the kingdom of God, and we are able to take possession of, wrestle with, overthrow, and extinguish the darts of the enemy.

By activating our faith, we are able to cross over from victim to victor. We move from the realm of testing to one of testimony.

Overcomer's Series

"My brethren, count it all joy when ye fall into divers temptations; Knowing this, that the trying of your faith worketh patience. But let patience have her perfect work, that ye may be perfect and entire, wanting nothing."

James 1:2-4

"And they overcame him by the blood of the Lamb, and by the word of their testimony; and they loved not their lives unto the death."

Revelation 12:11

The tests that we endure through the assaults of the enemy are designed to perfect us in the way of Christ Jesus. The path laid out for us is the same one walked by Christ himself.

Battling for the Light

> *"For we have not an high priest which cannot be touched with the feeling of our infirmities; but was in all points tempted like as we are, yet without sin."*
>
> Hebrews 4:15

Jesus walked the path of God to establish the foundation of our faith and now we are called to walk the path in Christ whom God hath sent.

> *"Jesus answered and said unto them, This is the work of God, that ye believe on him whom he hath sent."*
>
> John 6:29

> *'Whosoever believeth that Jesus is the Christ is born of God: and every one that loveth him that begat loveth him also that is begotten of him."*
>
> 1 John 5:1

Without the shield of faith, it is impossible for us to walk the path of God. Let us take up the shield of faith *above all* else for this is the work of God to believe on Jesus whom God hath sent!

Battling for the Light

Time to Examine Thyself

Do you have any doubts about God? Do you doubt he's able to do all that the Bible says he can do?

Are there situations where you believe you are better able to solve the problem or win the battle by yourself?

Do you run first and inquire of God later when things don't work out?

Where have you invested your faith? In God? In yourself? In men? Are there things in your life that cause you to be anxious? To worry or fret?

Overcomer's Series

Prayer

Father forgive me for sinning against you though worry, anxiety, and fear.

Renew the right spirit within me, one of confidence in my God so I can do great exploits (Daniel 11:32). There are situations in my life which have exhausted my faith, Lord increase my faith and help my unbelief (Romans 1:17 and Mark 9:24).

I desire to please you by believing in you all the way and standing firm in every situation. Amen.

DAY 8

IT'S TIME TO TAKE

"And take the helmet of salvation, and the sword of the Spirit, which is the word of God:"

Ephesians 6:17

In Ephesians 6:17, Paul uses the Greek word **dechomai** for the word **take**.

Dechomai means to take hold of, take with the hand, to receive or grant access to a visitor, to receive hospitality, or receive into one's family. It also means to learn, to take upon one's self, to embrace, give ear to, or to receive favorably. As we examine the word, further we learn that it means to educate, not to refuse, intercourse or friendship, and to bear and sustain.

The fact that Paul uses the word *dechomai* before the word helmet it denotes the active nature involved in taking up the helmet and using it. The word *dechomai* shows us that when we take up salvation, it opens the way for us to learn, bear up under pressure, and withstand (sustain) under constant assault.

Furthermore, it gives us an indication of what is involved with salvation. Salvation gives us the opportunity of friendship and intimate relationship with God through Jesus. It opens the way for us to be received into the family of God as it opens the way for Christ to visit with and lodge within us.

When we take the helmet of salvation, it opens the way for instruction and teaching, which comes through speaking via the Spirit of God. It fashions our ears so we will give ear to what we hear. Embedded in *dechomai's* meaning is the understanding that salvation should not be rejected but received upon ourselves.

Battling for the Light

Salvation is a gift from God, one He desires for us to accept so he can show and teach us his ways, and lead us in truth on the path of righteousness.

> *"For by grace are ye saved through faith; and that not of yourselves: it is the gift of God: Not of works, lest any man should boast."*

Ephesians 2:8-9 4

> *"Shew me thy ways, O Lord; teach me thy paths. Lead me in thy truth, and teach me: for thou art the God of my salvation; on thee do I wait all the day."*

Psalms 25:4-5

Overcomer's Series

Let's take upon ourselves the helmet of salvation. It's time to hear and receive instruction from the Lord. It's time for us to learn.

> *"Take my yoke upon you, and learn of me; for I am meek and lowly in heart: and ye shall find rest unto your souls."*
>
> Matthew 11:29
>
> *"For thou art my rock and my fortress; therefore for thy name's sake lead me, and guide me."*
>
> Psalms 31:3

Time to Examine Thyself

Do you carry the truth about your glorious salvation with you wherever you go? Do you know all the benefits provided for you with God's gift of salvation?

Do you allow salvations truth to guide and influence your thoughts, decisions, and acts at all times and in all situations?

Are you making the most use of your opportunity to live life as Christ's lives in the fullness of truth?

Prayer

Father, help me to live in your truth and in the fullness of your salvation.

Lord wash my mind and weed out all falsehood.

I thank you for opening the way of salvation to me. I praise you that I have been allowed to visit and to make my home with you as a citizen of heaven (Philippians 3:20-21) and you with me (John 14:23-24).

Lord teach and instruct me through the way of salvation. I will give ear to your counsel and embrace your wisdom, in Jesus name I pray, amen.

Battling for the Light

DAY 9

PRAYING ALWAYS

> *"Praying always with all prayer and supplication in the Spirit, and watching thereunto with all perseverance and supplication for all saints;"*
>
> Ephesians 6:18

In Ephesians 6:17, we are counseled to seize the helmet of salvation along with the sword of the Spirit, which is the Word of God. In verse 18, Paul further instructs us to pray always with all perseverance and supplication in the Spirit. What does this really mean?

Simply put, it's our responsibility to lift up and offer prayers to the advantage of all saints. Our prayers are to be in the kingdom (Colossians 1:13 and Philippians 3:20), directed toward God (Philippians 4:6), in regard to those who are in the body of Christ, and in reference to times and situations that believers are living in.

Things that we perceive by hearing or seeing are to influence our desire to pray for a strategy or solution that will bring about the will of God in the earth.

The word *always* in the verse is defined by three Greek words *en, kairos, and pas* and each one gives us insight into what *always* means to God.

En means in, with, by, into unto, towards, for, and among. *Karios* means due measure, a measure of time (large or small), opportune, seasonable, right, or limited time, limited period, what time brings, the things and events of time or the state of the times. *Pas* means individually, everyone, all, the whole, all things, everything, and collectively.

By these three words we know that prayers are to be offered by us, both individually and collectively. They are to be done in states of time, and they are to be directed toward or from within a specific place the kingdom of God.

Therefore, the cumulative meaning of *always* is that we are to communicate with, for, among, towards God using the mode of prayer. We are charged with praying long and short prayers, in season or when it is the most opportune time to pray effectively. We are to pray when things are brought to a crisis when events warrant our prayers because of the state of the times, or things that have come because of the time we are living in.

Our prayers are to also include our wishes (what we would like to see come to pass, Acts 12) according to the meaning of the Greek word for prayers.

Overcomer's Series

"Peter therefore was kept in prison: but prayer was made without ceasing of the church unto God for him. And when Herod would have brought him forth, the same night Peter was sleeping between two soldiers, bound with two chains: and the keepers before the door kept the prison. And, behold, the angel of the Lord came upon him, and a light shined in the prison: and he smote Peter on the side, and raised him up, saying, Arise up quickly. And his chains fell off from his hands. And the angel said unto him, Gird thyself, and bind on thy sandals. And so he did. And he saith unto him, Cast thy garment about thee, and follow me. And he went out, and followed him; and wist not that it was true which was done by the angel; but thought he saw a vision. When they were past the first and the second

Battling for the Light

ward, they came unto the iron gate that leadeth unto the city; which opened to them of his own accord: and they went out, and passed on through one street; and forthwith the angel departed from him. And when Peter was come to himself, he said, Now I know of a surety, that the Lord hath sent his angel, and hath delivered me out of the hand of Herod, and from all the expectation of the people of the Jews. And when he had considered the thing, he came to the house of Mary the mother of John, whose surname was Mark; where many were gathered together praying. And as Peter knocked at the door of the gate, a damsel came to hearken, named Rhoda. And when she knew Peter's voice, she opened not the gate for gladness, but ran in, and told how Peter stood before the gate. And they said unto her, Thou art mad. But she

Overcomer's Series

constantly affirmed that it was even so. Then said they, It is his angel. But Peter continued knocking: and when they had opened the door, and saw him, they were astonished. But he, beckoning unto them with the hand to hold their peace, declared unto them how the Lord had brought him out of the prison. And he said, Go shew these things unto James, and to the brethren. And he departed, and went into another place. The word of God does not leave us guessing as to who is responsible for lifting these prayers toward heaven. Each believer has a responsibility to pray individually, collectively, with the whole body of Christ, in all things and about everything."

Acts 12:5-17

Battling for the Light

Our prayers are to flow from our proper robing in the battle gear of God. The helmet of God ensures that our minds are not carnal or focused on temporal things. The sword of God ensures that our mouths will speak forth things that are life giving and eternal so they will come to pass.

> *"Death and life are in the power of the tongue: and they that love it shall eat the fruit thereof."*
>
> Proverbs 18:21

As believers, we are to be houses of prayer.

Overcomer's Series

"Even them will I bring to my holy mountain, and make them joyful in my house of prayer: their burnt offerings and their sacrifices shall be accepted upon mine altar; for mine house shall be called an house of prayer for all people."

Isaiah 56:7

If we refuse to pray then we are like robbers or thieves who take for their own interests and refuse to be a blessing and give or make an investment for the benefit of others.

It's a selfish act to withhold prayers, for it shows that we are only concerned with our own self-interests. Desiring to be blessed but not willing to be a blessing to the body of Christ or to sow righteousness and life in the earth.

Battling for the Light

"And said unto them, It is written, My house shall be called the house of prayer; but ye have made it a den of thieves."

Matthew 21:13

Are you willing to be a house of prayer? Are you willing to pray always?

Overcomer's Series

Time to Examine Thyself

Are you preoccupied or consumed with yourself? Are the only problems that matter to you those of your family or yourself?

When you pray for others, do you have a hurry up spirit? Are you impatient when listening to someone else's troubles? Is all well with the world once all is well with you and your household?

If you know, you are self-absorbed and self-focused take time to ask the Lord for the grace to die to self so that you can fully live in Christ Jesus. If you feel that you are in danger of falling into the snare of selfishness, ask God to give you discernment, strength, and wisdom so that you will not be a mockery in the earth.

Battling for the Light

Prayer

Oh Lord, my God and my help, hear me as my soul cries out to you.

Father, selfishness is knocking at my door and desires to consume me. I ask you to be mighty and strong on my behalf. Give me the grace to resist the enemy so that he will flee from me.

Lord, I desire to be a watchman on the wall, I long to be my brother's keeper, I desire to help cover him with spiritual prayers, feed him with spiritual meat (truth), and set him free from the bondage of the enemy.

Teach me how to pray effective prayers, which will avail much in the lives of others as it advances your kingdom. Thank you for hearing and answering my prayer, in Jesus name, amen.

Overcomer's Series

DAY 10

CHILDREN OF LIGHT

"For ye were sometimes darkness, but now are ye light in the Lord: walk as children of light:"

Ephesians 5:8

As believers in Jesus Christ, we are to walk in light, as Jesus is in the light (1 John 1:7). We are charged with the responsibility to be children of light (1 Thessalonians 5:5) because we were delivered from the bowels of darkness (Ephesians 5:8).

We are lights in the world, representatives of a Holy God (Matthew 5:14-16), and are ambassadors of the city of God. But what does this really mean to be lights in the world?

Battling for the Light

The first mention of light in the Bible is in Genesis 1:3 and it comes from the Hebrew word ***owr***, which means light of day, daybreak, morning light, light of life, light of prosperity, light of instruction. The root meaning of ***owr*** is to become light, to shine, to give light, to lighten the eyes, to make the face shine, or to become bright.

Woven into the meaning of ***light*** is the notion of life, prosperity, instruction, brightness, and transformation. It involves light breaking through the darkness or obstruction as in the breaking forth of a flower through the soil. The act of learning new ways of living or being as one sheds old beliefs, ideas, and notions. It is moving from a place of lack or poverty into a place of abundance or prosperity.

As Children of light, we are to pierce through darkness by the grace of Christ. The darkness might be in our attitudes, beliefs, customs, rituals, philosophies, works, relationships, body, health, acts, speech, etc. No matter where the darkness resides, we are to pierce it through with light, the area should be claimed for Jesus who is the ***"light of the world."***

> *"Then spake Jesus again unto them, saying, I am the light of the world: he that followeth me shall not walk in darkness, but shall have the light of life."*
>
> John 8:12

As we walk in the light of Jesus we too will be transformed into greater lights (Genesis 1:16, Acts 26:18, Isaiah 9:2) resulting in our eyes being lightened, our understanding enlightened, and our countenances brightened (Ephesians 1:18-19).

In each of us, God has kindled a desire for light (Psalms 37:4, Ecclesiastes 3:11), for we responded to his invitation to come out of darkness, but it's up to us to decide whether we will become fully illuminated by the power of God.

Battling for the Light

Walking in the light is to be exposed to view, to appear, or to be seen. It is being one who brings forth light, a dispenser of light. It is to facilitate growth, for in order for vegetation to grow it requires light (2 Corinthians 3:18, Romans 1:17). It is possessing the power of understanding of moral and spiritual truth.

> *"That the God of our Lord Jesus Christ, the Father of glory, may give unto you the spirit of wisdom and revelation in the knowledge of him:"*
>
> Ephesians 1:17
>
> *"Get wisdom, get understanding: forget it not; neither decline from the words of my mouth."*
>
> Proverbs 4:5

Overcomer's Series

Walking in the light of Jesus also means to make ones thoughts known through declaration or the use of speech. This is exactly what God did through Jesus the Word of God.

Jesus the Light of the World came to declare the message of God. He made known to us the thoughts and declarations of the Father. As we follow his example, we too will make known the message of our Savior and Lord. We will be willing to share our testimonies, thoughts, and feelings toward our God. We will make declarations about who our God is, what he has done, and what he will do.

As children of light, we will be seen and our lives will be on open display as we live in the light. We can refuse to exist in total light. We can opt to remain in the shadows, hiding behind our fig leaves, lurking in the outskirts, and held in the familiar embrace of darkness (Genesis 3:7).

Light is active and forceful. Light has the ability to take on darkness and

Battling for the Light

come out the victor each and every time, even in the midst of evidence to the contrary (John 19, Acts 7:54-60, 1 John 3:8, Luke 12:51-53).

Light divides, it separates, and it marks a line of clear distinction between opposing forces, entities, or groups.

> *"I am come a light into the world, that whosoever believeth on me should not abide in darkness."*
>
> John 12:46
>
> *"But if we walk in the light, as he is in the light, we have fellowship one with another, and the blood of Jesus Christ his Son cleanseth us from all sin."*
>
> 1 John 1:7

Walk in the light. Choose to battle all darkness. Allow God to complete his illuminating work in you. Radiant beauty is your birthright; don't throw it away for fleshly pleasures (Genesis 25:29-34). As you stand for light, you overcome darkness.

> *"Wherefore take unto you the whole armour of God, that ye may be able to withstand in the evil day, and having done all, to stand."*
>
> Ephesians 6:13

Battling for the Light

Time to Examine Thyself

Take a few moments to ask Holy Spirit to expose any areas of darkness in your life. List all the areas, that come to mind. It could be a foul mouth, ungodly behaviors, spiteful thoughts, envying eyes, worry, fear of the future, loving others more than you love Christ, selfishness, or a host of other things.

Are you willing to allow Christ to lead you fully into the light?

Prayer

My Father and my wonderful God, anoint me with courage to face the ugly side of myself.

Help me to call sin, sin. Help me to expose all darkness in my life to the light of Jesus.

It is my desire to exist, live, and walk in the light of Jesus. Though I fall, help me to get up. Help me when I miss the mark to repent quickly and to continue on the path laid out before me.

Overcomer's Series

Make me bright, beautiful, and pleasing unto you. Hear my heart's desire . . . . in Jesus name, amen.

Battling for the Light

DAY 11

LET YOUR LIGHT SO SHINE

"Let your light so shine before men, that they may see your good works, and glorify your Father which is in heaven."

Matthew 5:16

In Matthew 5:14-16, Jesus used several illustrations about light, in order to convey a fundamental truth, which is; we are to operate at all times as **bringers of light**. We are citizens of God's holy city, and as such we are candles lit for the purpose of providing light to all those around us.

In every conceivable context, Jesus pierced the eye, mind, and hearts of men with the light of truth releasing the knowledge of God unto them. His assignment was to make known to men the truth about God, so that they would gain understanding.

Overcomer's Series

"The fear of the LORD is the beginning of wisdom: and the knowledge of the holy is understanding."

Proverbs 9:10

"All things are delivered unto me of my Father: and no man knoweth the Son, but the Father; neither knoweth any man the Father, save the Son, and he to whomsoever the Son will reveal him."

Matthew 11:27

Understanding comes from knowing God through the mouth of wisdom, which is Christ.

"But of him are ye in Christ Jesus, who of God is made unto us wisdom, and righteousness, and sanctification, and redemption:"

1 Corinthians 1:30

Battling for the Light

"For the LORD giveth wisdom: out of his mouth cometh knowledge and understanding."

Proverbs 2:6

Therefore, it is expected that as purveyors of light we too are to become mouthpieces of wisdom that release light unto those we come in contact, so that they will have an opportunity to acquire a knowledge of God which will lead their gaining of understanding.

How can men gain knowledge if we hide our light? How can they acquire understanding if we fail to speak words of wisdom because of fear or intimidation?

We are called to be a city set on a hill or a candle that gives light to all who reside in the house. It is in this manner that we are to shed light so that others can find their way out of darkness. Our light is to be a prominent feature of our being. Why? Because . . .

Overcomer's Series

"This then is the message which we have heard of him, and declare unto you, that God is light, and in him is no darkness at all."

1 John 1:5

"Then spake Jesus again unto them, saying, I am the light of the world: he that followeth me shall not walk in darkness, but shall have the light of life."

John 8:12

God is pure light; there is no darkness in him. Christ is the light of the world, and we have been drawn out of darkness so we can become children of light!

"Ye are all the children of light, and the children of the day: we are not of the night, nor of darkness."

1 Thessalonians 5:5

Battling for the Light

"For ye were sometimes darkness, but now are ye light in the Lord: walk as children of light:"

Ephesians 5:8

"While ye have light, believe in the light, that ye may be the children of light. These things spake Jesus, and departed, and did hide himself from them."

John 12:36

Are you ready to shine with radiant brilliancy as child of light?

Overcomer's Series

Time to Examine Thyself

Take a few minutes today to examine your life. Are there areas in your life where darkness still lurks?

Are there attitudes or actions, that dim the light of Christ in you? Are there relationships you should not have or conversations you should not indulge in?

If so, now is the right time to expose it to the light of Christ. Chase every form of darkness from your life. Free your heart, mind, body, soul and being from the influence of the enemy. Try to establish healthy life giving relationships.

Prayer

My Father and my God, thank you for your kindness toward me. Thank you that you have given me yet another day on the land of the living. Thank you that you have blessed me with the opportunity to expose all darkness to the light of Christ.

Battling for the Light

Forgive me where I have allowed darkness to influence my thinking, behavior, opinions, judgments, and conversation. Create in me a clean heart and renew the right spirit within me.

Father, I want my light to shine before men so that all that I do, think, and say will bring glory to You.

I praise you because I know you are faithful to complete all that you start. In Jesus name, I pray, amen.

Overcomer's Series

DAY 12

CANDLES HIDE NOT

> *"No man, when he hath lighted a candle, putteth it in a secret place, neither under a bushel, but on a candlestick, that they which come in may see the light."*
>
> Luke 11:33

As believers in Jesus Christ we have been lit by the flame of God. His intent is that we remain radiant lights in a dark world. We are to shine forth the light of life, hope, love, and obedience, as we establish the will of God on the earth.

When we abide in Christ, we will do what pleases God. Our works will testify that we are of Christ (1 Corinthians 3:23) and are therefore ***truly*** sons of God.

Battling for the Light

Luke 11:33, makes a profound and enlightening statement. Absolutely no man, not even one, would ever light a candle and lay it down in a vault, hidden away from those who need light. When a candle is lit, it has one purpose, which is to provide light!

Therefore, as the lights of God though the work of Jesus, we are to expose those around us to light so that they may see as well. We are to pierce their eyes with the light of understanding (Psalms 119:130, Ephesians 1:18), to prick them with the light of divine wisdom (1 Corinthians 1:30), and confound them with the light of our obedience (John 14:15).

Our speech is to baffle them (Ephesians 4:29, Colossians 4:6), our actions to influence them (2 Corinthians 3:2-3), and our testimony of Christ is to draw them (John 12:32).

Overcomer's Series

If we choose to hide our lights, it will speak out against us for it is an act of treason. We are citizens of the kingdom of light. We are called to be children of light. When we hide our candle for whatever reason we have chosen to operate as a rebel against the cause and purpose of God.

When we choose to keep our mouths closed when we should speak, "Thus sayeth the Lord." Or when we take an action even though we know it is wrong, just because everyone else says it is okay. Or when we excuse a lie, by calling it a little white lie we have in reality handed over our victory through Christ to the enemy.

Therefore, our choices will witness against us as will Holy Spirit who resides within us.

> *"Know ye not that ye are the temple of God, and that the Spirit of God dwelleth in you?"*
>
> 1 Corinthians 3:16

Battling for the Light

For this reason, we should choose to speak, act, and operate at all times as ambassadors of light.

> *"Now then we are ambassadors for Christ, as though God did beseech you by us: we pray you in Christ's stead, be ye reconciled to God."*
>
> 2 Corinthians 5:20
>
> *"God forbid: yea, let God be true, but every man a liar; as it is written, That thou mightest be justified in thy sayings, and mightest overcome when thou art judged."*
>
> Romans 3:4

When we choose to shine our lights, God will preserve our whole spirit, soul, and body blameless until Christ returns.

Overcomer's Series

"And the very God of peace sanctify you wholly; and I pray God your whole spirit and soul and body be preserved blameless unto the coming of our Lord Jesus Christ."

1 Thessalonians 5:23

Are you willing to pierce the darkness with the light?

Battling for the Light

Time to Examine Thyself

Today take stock of how your light has shun for Christ. Have you been a bright beacon for the Lord? Have you projected his love, spread his hope, and shed his truth?

Has your life upheld the laws of the kingdom of God? Have you extended the mercy and grace to others as it was extended to you? Do you forgive as God forgives you?

In whatever areas you have fallen short, ask Christ to illuminate the way for you to transition from dimness into the glorious reality of his light.

As you pray for yourself, pray that he will use you in greater measure to give light to those who desire to come out of darkness and enter into the wonders of his love.

Overcomer's Series

Prayer

Blessed be the Lord my God who has called me to be a beacon of light on the earth. Thank you for the privilege of being a child of light.

Father I glorify your name. Lord I confess that my light has not shun the way it ought and for that, I repent and ask for your forgiveness.

You have called me to be a light in dark places, to project the gloriousness of your nature.

Father help me that my life will be one that is pleasing to you. Guide my words, influence my actions, set my course, intensity my light, set your word in my heart, and lead me by your Spirit.

May my life bring you honor and glory, I pray, amen.

Battling for the Light

DAY 13

WHILE YE HAVE LIGHT

"While ye have light, believe in the light, that ye may be the children of light. These things spake Jesus, and departed, and did hide himself from them."

John 12:36

While ye have light . . . what did Jesus mean by those opening words? Why would he speak such things to his followers? Was the sun going to stop shinning? Was darkness getting ready to cover the earth with a blanket of blackness? Where the inhabitants getting ready to enter an ice age?

Overcomer's Series

The light that Jesus was referring to was the light of spiritual purity, the brightness of God's glory, and the sound reasoning of the mind of God. In essence himself.

Christ the fullness of the light of God was going to be on the earth for only a set a period of time, a period that no one knew except for God.

Jesus was issuing a warning that light would be around for a preordained season and then darkness would come. He was informing the hearers that **NOW** was the season to grow in the light, to be impacted by the light, and to be shaped by the truth and knowledge of light.

Fortunately, for us we are still in the *now* season where we can still grow in the light of God through Christ Jesus. But the time when darkness will take over is swiftly approaching. It is closer to us than it was when Jesus originally spoke those words to his followers.

Battling for the Light

Therefore, his message is even more urgent for us today.

We should take his counsel to heart. We should ask ourselves, are we truly walking in the light? Are we allowing spiritual purity to rule in our members?

Are our loins covered by truth, our hearts protected with the breastplate of righteousness, and our feet adorned with the gospel of peace (Ephesians 6:12-15)? Have we taken up the shield of faith, and placed on our heads the helmet of salvation (Ephesians 6:16)? Do we carry the sword of the Spirit daily (Ephesians 6:17).

Darkness desires to lure us from the fold of God; it desires to sift us like wheat, and to seduce us into leaving our first love. Our only hope is to remain faithful to Christ, to believe in the light, and to desire increased light as children of light.

Overcomer's Series

While we have light, let us be willing to continue in the path of God, which leads to increased light, thorough the power of Jesus.

Battling for the Light

Time to Examine Thyself

Today let us examine ourselves for areas of darkness. How many have you identified? What do you plan to do about these areas, which tarnish the glory of God within you?

Are you willing to go further, to dig deeper? Inquire of the Lord what areas of darkness he sees, but only if you are willing to follow his instructions on how to get rid of them.

Sometimes we need increased faith to deal with troublesome areas in our lives. Sometimes we need increase strength. At other times, we need the peace of God to encamp round about us so that we do not lose our minds.

And, still there are other times when we need to feel the reality of God's unshakable love hugging us. Whatever it is that you need in order to believe and walk in the light so that you can become a full-fledged child of light ask for it!

Overcomer's Series

Prayer

Lord, I need your help. I want to be a child of light. But I do not know what I need to do. Identify areas of darkness in me. Give me the strength and determination to stay the course until your work is completed in me.

Remove every weed from my life, the weed of ignorance, fear, intimidation. The lack of knowledge, and those weeds of lust, pride, remove all negativity that the enemy has planted to interfere with healthy spiritual growth.

Lord fertilize me with your love, water me with your peace, and increase my faith. Keep hope alive within me. Help me not to look at the circumstance or situation but to keep my eyes on you. Lift me and sustain me.

Father, please get the fullness of your glory out of my life, in Jesus name, amen.

DAY 14

YE ARE ALL CHILDREN OF LIGHT

"Ye are all the children of light, and the children of the day: we are not of the night, nor of darkness."

1 Thessalonians 5:5

What a wonderful thing it is to be children of the light! We exist in the light of Christ. We are present in heavenly realms in the city of light.

In 1 Thessalonians 5:5, our nature and position in the light is made clear. Paul uses the power of words to draw a clear line of distinction between whom we are in Jesus and who we are not.

Overcomer's Series

As children of light, we are to love the daytime and avoid walking in the darkness of the enemy in all things, at all times. Why? Because we are the offspring of the Father of light. And because of this simple fact we are to restrict the activity of darkness from manifesting in our lives.

We are called to emit light and reflect the spiritual purity of God. In those around us. To encourage them to live and walk in the light of Jesus. We are public spectacles that represent God to the world. When we walk in darkness or have fellowship with children of the night, it misrepresents God. It causes onlookers to get the wrong perception of who God is and of his standards.

God has made our duty simple. He has carved out a path upon which we are to travel. We do not have to reinvent the wheel nor do we need to lay a new foundation. As Christ walked the path of God so are we. As he upheld the Word of God so are we.

Battling for the Light

We are not children of light if we occasionally like to stroll in the shadows or we hide our activities in the dark.

True children of light love the light, and welcome their activities to be viewed and observed in the light where all can see.

Are you a lover of light? Or do you occasionally lurk in the shadows?

Overcomer's Series

Time to Examine Thyself

As we go through life, there are situations and circumstances, which may cause us to make the wrong decision. Fear can cause us to lie or doubt. Worry can cause us to make the wrong profession of faith. But as children of light we are not ignorant of the times when we have fallen.

What do we do when we recognize we have sinned? How should we rectify the matter? Are we comfortable with sin? Or are we repentant?

Those who love light will be uncomfortable walking in darkness. The children of the day will fix themselves in the presence of God. If by chance, they slip into the shadows they will quickly find their way out before they are engulfed by darkness.

Today take time to examine your life. Are you a lover of light? Are you fixed in light as a child of the day? Or are there areas in your life which need to be exposed to the light of the Lord?

Battling for the Light

Prayer

Father, I thank you that you have called me to be a child of light. Establish me as a child of the day. Help me to despise the darkness.

When I slip and fall, cause me to be aware and help my heart to be repentant. It is my desire for the enemy to have nothing in me. Help me to abide in the light of Jesus, forever I pray, amen.

Overcomer's Series

DAY 15

LIGHT SHINETH IN DARKNESS

"And the light shineth in darkness; and the darkness comprehended it not."

John 1:5

Jesus Christ is the brightest light that has ever existed. He pierced the very heart of darkness and over powered it. Jesus made an open display of the devil. He made a mockery of his lies. He exposed them for what they were, seeds of deception engineered to cause men to fall and to lead men into destruction.

Battling for the Light

Let us be clear, there is no other light more radiant than the light of Christ! His light is brilliant, unquenchable, and unstoppable. The light of Jesus exposes everything and lacks nothing!

The light of Christ accomplishes several tasks, it brings us forth into light, it causes us to shine, and it transforms and positions us to shed light to those around us.

Paul said it best in Ephesians, we were sometimes in darkness, but now through the work of Christ, we are in the light of the Lord.

> *"For ye were sometimes darkness, but now are ye light in the Lord: walk as children of light: (For the fruit of the Spirit is in all goodness and righteousness and truth;)"*
>
> Ephesians 5:8-9

Overcomer's Series

The darkness, which covered us, also tarnished, soiled, and dimmed us. But the light of God pierced our eyes, causing us to see the true condition of our lives, and to realize our need for a savior.

Our profession of faith and acceptance of Jesus Christ facilitated the cleansing process of God. This process is like the polishing of a gem, which was covered with dirt, muck, and debris.

> *"Wash me throughly from mine iniquity, and cleanse me from my sin."*
>
> Psalms 51:2

As Christ ignites truth in our heart, his light continues to open our eyes, and leads us into deeper truth where we grow in beauty, brightness, and magnificence.

Battling for the Light

As we submit to the procedure of God, he starts to move us as chess pieces on a board, placing us in the optimal position for us to reflect his light, to shed light, and to dispel darkness. The objective is to checkmate the enemy at each turn. Light is preordained to win.

> *"Ye are the light of the world. A city that is set on an hill cannot be hid."*
>
> Matthew 5:14

Overcomer's Series

Time to Examine Thyself

Today, take time to reflect on our fifteen-day journey as we battled for the light. Have you identified areas in your life that need more work? That needs to be exposed to more light?

Are you more determined than ever to battle for your birthright as a child of light? Have you dealt with feelings of rejection and inadequacy, which may have attacked you because you are a peculiar person in Jesus?

Are you settled in your heart and mind that it is acceptable if the world does not understand you?

If there are still areas in which you are struggling, take time to lift them up to the Lord. He is your sufficiency! Remember that he has already approved you.

Battling for the Light

Prayer

Father I bless your name; I glorify you for you are a good and merciful God. Abundant in patience, overflowing in love, and eternally kind to your children.

Thank you for identifying in me areas in which battles are raging. The enemy is contending with me, trying to snuff out the light of Christ in me.

Father strengthen me. Help me to wrestle all forces of the enemy down, subduing them under the Lordship of Jesus Christ. Cause your light to shine through me. Make it pierce the darkness, let it overtake and overthrow the evil one, in Jesus name.

Overcomer's Series

Father I celebrate you, for victory is already mine through the completed work of Jesus. As I lend my hand and submit my will to your process, cause victory to manifest continually in my life. May your light pierce the eyes of those who observe me. May their eyes be enlighten, their hearts transformed, and their minds engaged in the pursuit of truth, in Jesus name, amen.

CONCLUSION

Brethren let us not be deceived; we are in a war of eternal significance. The Devil is determined to separate us from our eternal destiny. He fights dirty, using our flesh, willing vessels, and all manner of enticements to seduce or intimidate us into leaving God. Because we are born in sin and shaped in iniquity, Satan seems to have an advantage over us. He knows what brings us pleasure and what causes annoyance. He enjoys causing us to sin so he can accuse us before God. His objective, is **division**.

But as crafty as he is and in spite of his apparent head start in our lives God will make a mockery of the enemy and his works in our lives. It does not matter if Satan has had a 50-year head start or just two years. Jesus the mighty ram will battle all contenders for the hand of his bride whom he loves.

Overcomer's Series

There is however, a condition . . . we must remain in him. Remaining faithful can be challenging but the grace of Jesus is sufficient, it will cause us to stand. As warriors of light, we have a responsibility to brighten the spot of the world in which we reside. Once the light of Christ is firmly established in us we will be purveyors (spreaders) of light.

The Devil has managed to keep many of us out of the battle through fear, intimidation, feelings of guilt, condemnation, deception, and false doctrine. It's time to tear down his strongholds and to set him to flight.

Are you ready to run to the battle? Are you ready to chase the enemy of your soul away? ***Are you willing to expose all to the light?***

Battling for the Light

> *"And it came to pass, when the Philistine arose, and came and drew nigh to meet David, that David hasted, and ran toward the army to meet the Philistine."*
>
> 1 Samuel 17:48

If you don't deal with him, he will deal with you!

> *"And that they may recover themselves out of the snare of the devil, who are taken captive by him at his will."*
>
> 2 Timothy 2:26

Why not recover yourself today?

Overcomer's Series

www.ingramcontent.com/pod-product-compliance
Lightning Source LLC
Chambersburg PA
CBHW040925190426
43197CB00033B/103